CBD HEMP OIL

The Complete Beginner's Guide on how to use CBD Hemp Oil

TABLE OF CONTENTS

- Introduction 4
- Terminology 5
- CHAPTER 1 7
  - WHAT IS CBD HEMP OIL 7
  - BRIEF HISTORY OF CBD 9
- CHAPTER 2 15
  - WHERE DOES CBD HEPM OIL COME FROM 15
  - SOURCING CBD 38
  - CBD/THC COMPARISON 41
- CHAPTER 3 43
  - BENEFITS AND EFFECTS OF CBD HEMP OIL 44
  - SIDE EFFECTS OF CBD HEPM OIL 58
- CHAPTER 4 65
  - CBD HEPM OIL BUYER'S GUIDE 65
  - CBD HEMP OIL DIFFEFERNT PRODUCTS 67
  - HOW TO BUY CBD OIL – WATCH OUT FOR THESE 3 TRAPS! 78
- CHAPTER 5 82
  - CBD HEP OIL PHARMACOKINETICS 82
  - CANCER 84
  - EPILEPSY 89
  - PSYCHOSIS 92
  - ANXIETY 95
- CONCLUSION 105

☞Copyright 2018 by Tom Berfelo - All rights reserved.

This document is geared towards providing exact and reliable information in regards to the topic and issue covered. The publication is sold with the idea that the publisher is not required to render accounting, officially permitted, or otherwise, qualified services. If advice is necessary, legal or professional, a practiced individual in the profession should be ordered.

- From a Declaration of Principles which was accepted and approved equally by a Committee of the American Bar Association and a Committee of Publishers and Associations.

In no way is it legal to reproduce, duplicate, or transmit any part of this document in either electronic means or in printed format. Recording of this publication is strictly prohibited and any storage of this document is not allowed unless with written permission from the publisher. All rights reserved.

The information provided herein is stated to be truthful and consistent, in that any liability, in terms of inattention or otherwise, by any usage or abuse of any policies, processes, or directions contained within is the solitary and utter responsibility of the recipient reader. Under no circumstances will any legal responsibility or blame be held against the publisher for any reparation, damages, or monetary loss due to the information herein, either directly or indirectly.

Respective authors own all copyrights not held by the publisher.

The information herein is offered for informational purposes solely, and is universal as so. The presentation of the information is without contract or any type of guarantee assurance.

The trademarks that are used are without any consent, and the publication of the trademark is without permission or backing by the trademark owner. All trademarks and brands within this book are for clarifying purposes only and are the owned by the owners themselves, not affiliated with this document.

INTRODUCTION

Cannabis sativa, from which hemp and marijuana are derived, has been a source of medicinal, industrial, and recreational commodities for centuries. The term "hemp" refers primarily to cannabis grown as an agricultural crop and is characterized by cannabis plants that are low in delta-9 THC (tetrahydrocannabinol), the main psychoactive ingredient in marijuana. Although more than 30 nations worldwide grow hemp as an agricultural commodity, in the United States, production is strictly controlled under existing drug enforcement laws.

As of January 2015, twenty states have passed legislation favorable to hemp cultivation. The main obstacles facing the potential U.S. market are the government drug policies and Drug Enforcement Administration (DEA) concerns that the commercial cultivation could increase the likelihood of covert production of high- Tetrahydrocannabinol (THC) cannabis varieties or inadvertent cross pollination, complicating DEA surveillance.

In recent years, scientific knowledge regarding the composition and health benefits of edible hemp products has significantly increased. Hemp seed oil has been promoted as a good source of nutritious omega-6 and omega-3 polyunsaturated acids, and may be a cleaner, more sustainable alternative to fish oil. While hemp seed oil has been shown to have high nutritive value, it is generally believed that it may also afford other beneficial qualities.

Terminology

Cannabis. Cannabis is the preferred designation of the plant Cannabis sativa, Cannabis indica, and of minor significance, Cannabis ruderalis. According to the 1961 United Nations Single Convention on Narcotic Drugs, cannabis is defined as "the flowering or fruiting tops of the cannabis plant (excluding the seeds and leaves when not accompanied by the tops) from which the resin has not been extracted, by whatever name they may be designated." Cannabis resin means "separated resin, whether crude or purified, obtained from the cannabis plant". These definitions are narrower than the botanical definition and as a consequence, certain parts of the plant are not under international control. The term cannabis will be used instead of marijuana, or other names indigenous to local cultures, unless there is a need to refer to a specific phrase, e.g. medical marijuana ballot initiatives. Its use for medicinal, ritual or recreational purposes results from the actions of cannabinoids in the cannabis plant. These compounds also produce the unintended adverse consequences of cannabis.

Cannabinoids : Cannabinoids are basically derived from three sources: (a) Phytocannabinoids are cannabinoid compounds produced by plants Cannabis sativa or Cannabis indica; (b)Endocannabinoids are neurotransmitters produced in the brain or in peripheral tissues, and act on cannabinoid receptors; (c) Synthetic cannabinoids, synthesized in the laboratory, are structurally analogous to phytocannabinoids or endocannabinoids and act by similar biological mechanisms.

CHAPTER 1

WHAT IS CBD HEMP OIL

CBD (Cannabidoil) is a chemical compound known as a cannabidoid, and the second most abundant source in the hemp plant (about 40%), from which it is extracted and separated. The first most common source in hemp is THC (Tetrahydrocannabinol), which is an intoxicant and is used recreationally around the world as an illegal drug. CBD and THC are NOT the same, although they both come from the same plant. You cannot get 'high' from CBD hemp (with low levels of THC), nor from CBD oil products (which contain no THC at all).

CBD is extracted from hemp and can be used as an oil, with a growing international body of science pointing to its nutritional and health benefits.

Cannabidiol (CBD) is a chemical compound that comes from the hemp plant. It is one of over 85 unique compounds found in hemp, known as cannabinoids. While its exact benefits and effects are still being researched, it is interesting to note that the United States Department of Health and Human Services holds a patent titled 'Cannabinoids as Antioxidants and Neuroprotectants', which claims that:

- ❖ "Nonpsychoactive cannabinoids, such as cannabidiol, are particularly advantageous to use because they avoid toxicity that is encountered with psychoactive cannabinoids at high doses useful in the method of the present invention."

Cannabinoids, which can be either consumed (phytocannabinoids) or produced naturally by the body (endocannabinoid), are chemical compounds that interact with the body's central regulatory system (the endocannabinoid system). This system is known to manage homeostasis and affect bodily processes such as appetite, mood and sleep. CBD is an example of a phytocannabinoid. Although our bodies can naturally produce its own endocannabinoids that bind to cannabinoid receptors in both the central nervous system and the peripheral nervous system, phytocannabinoids help to kickstart our central regulatory system and provide powerful benefits.

BRIEF HISTORY OF CBD

The roots of Cannabidiol (CBD) extend back thousands of years; to the end of the first ice age, Archaeological finds suggest that the source plant for the CBD compound, Cannabis Sativa, was likely one of the first agricultural crops planted by early man. In fact, growing Cannabis Sativa, something we tend to think of as modern, is often associated with the birth of agriculture 12,000 to 10,000 years ago.

The astronomer Carl Sagan an icon of scientific credibility, put forth the possibility that Cannabis may have been world's first agricultural crop, leading to the development of civilization itself. Looking at time lines, it is clear that cannabis plants have been integral to mankind since earliest times.

Food, Medicine and More

Cannabis plants are exceptionally versatile. Both the seeds and cannabis oil were used for food in China as early as 6,000 BCE. Two thousand years later, in 4,000 BCE, there is evidence of textiles made from hemp (cannabis) used in both China and Turkestan.

The influence of the plant seems to have been global. In 850, the Vikings transported hemp rope and seeds to Iceland, and by the year 900, Arabs were learning techniques for making paper from hemp. By 1000 (1015 years ago), Italians were using ropes made of hemp on their sailing ships.

Today, consumers are primarily interested in the healthful properties of cannabis compounds, and there is a long thread of cannabis applications for healing running through all eras of history. Stories about the healing properties of hemp (cannabis) mention Greek philosophers, Herodotus, Napoleon and other legendary figures. The physician for Nero's army, for example, included cannabis in his medical inventory. In 1563, the medicinal benefits of cannabis were discussed in a report by Portuguese physician Garcia da Orta. A few years later, China's Li Shih-Chen documented the antibiotic and anti-nausea effects of cannabis.

A Mandated Crop

In contrast to today's modern restrictions of growing Cannabis Sativa, England's King Henry VIII actually fined farmers if they do not raise hemp for industrial use. This was in 1533. Less than one hundred years later, settlers in Jamestown, Virginia--the New World----began growing hemp plants for hemp's unusually strong fiber. Once the plant demonstrated its usefulness, it became illegal to NOT grow hemp in Virginia.

By 1850, Cannabis was added to list of The U.S.Pharmacopeia, a respected compendium of Medicines and Dietary Supplements. That same year, marijuana was used throughout United States as a medicinal drug and could easily be purchased in pharmacies and general stores. This lasted until about 1915.

Seeds of Change

According to the North America Industrial Hemp Council (NAIHC), growing Cannabis Sativa, even for industrial hemp purposes, has been effectively prohibited in the United States since the 1950s. Things may be changing however. The explosion of interest in hemp derived compounds and products, most especially Cannabidiol (CBD), has motivated farmers and advocates across the U.S. to lobby for restoring the legal status of hemp as an agricultural crop in all 50 states. Currently, only a portion of U.S. states can grow hemp (Cannabis Sativa) legally, including Colorado the home of DiscoverCBD.com.

We are committed to providing you with the best information, as well as the best products. If you have a question or comment regarding CBD, let us know, and we will respond right away. In the meantime, sign up for our newsletters and visit our website regularly for the latest updates on research, legislation, and other news impacting your access to Cannabidiol.

Cannabidiol (CBD) has been enjoying increasing amounts of attention as people learn more about its incredible possibilities as a supplement. With so many articles and research studies being written about CBD, you might think that this consumable is a recent discovery. It is true that many of the CBD extraction and packaging methods use cutting-edge technologies but the use of CBD in its hemp oil form goes back farther than most people realize.

In the 2010's the public began to see what a profound effect CBD oil could have treating a variety of life threatening aliments, especially in children. A prime example of this is a young family from Missoula Montana, using CBD oil to treat their 20 month old son, Cash Hyde, who had been diagnosed with brain cancer in 2010. Hyde's condition was worsening and his tumor inoperable. After exhausting every treatment option, including 30 rounds of intensive radiation, Ketamine, Methadone and Morphine treatments, the Hyde family had hit their limit. Nothing had worked. In an effort to give his small child some relief, his father did what was thought to be "crazy"at the time, and gave him a highly concentrated cannabis extract, not knowing 0what else to do. After the first treatment, Hyde's State IV brain tumor had shrunk. Although it was considered unorthodox, Mike

Hyde was applauded by medical professionals and even spoke with the press in hopes of shedding the light on how CBD oil is literally a lifesaver.

Cash Hyde lived for another two and a half years, passing away after the State of Montana made a change in legislation that impaired the family from easily accessing the cannabis oil their son needed.

Perhaps the most prolific case of CBD oil and it's success is the 2013 story that achieved national press. Charolette Figi is a 3 year old Colorado girl who suffered 300 grand mal seizures every week. Like the Hyde family, her parents thought they had tried everything, including a heavy regime of pharmaceutical drugs and painful procedures that still did not ease her condition. Her parents had watched a documentary of one of the first medical marijuana dispensaries in California centered around testing their strains of CBD and other cannaboid content. The California center testing was one of the first public assertions that cannabis was safe to ingest and use for a variety of medical purposes. CBD rich oil was able to treat 99% of the young girls seizures, and CNN aired a 2013 special on marijuana and it medicinal effects.

These are just a few specific instances that show how effective CBD oil can be, laying the groundwork for CBD oil being recognized as a justifiable medicine for a variety of ailments. As a result, many states are passing legislation rapidly allowing CBD oil to be used in numerous clinical studies as treatment plans. Research continues to back up it legitimacy and programs are being funded globally to continue the studies.

CHAPTER 2

WHERE DOES CBD HEPM OIL COME FROM

What are the best plants for extracting and making high quality CBD-rich oil? Marijuana, industrial hemp, both?

Let's cut through the legal mumbo jumbo, the obfuscating nomenclature, and the marketing hype and let's look at what's really out there for sourcing CBD-rich oil.

In the cannabis world there are two types of plants, broadly categorized — hemp plants and drug plants. Hemp plants include plants grown for fiber and plants grown for seed oil. Drug plants include euphoric THC-rich plants and non-euphoric CBD-rich plants.

The key difference between hemp plants and drug plants is resin content. Most hemp plants are low-resin plants. Drug plants are high-resin plants. Industrial hemp varieties are typically a low-resin agricultural crop, grown from pedigree seed, with about one hundred tall, skinny plants per square meter, machine harvested and manufactured into a multitude of products.

Drug plants are a high-resin horticultural crop, typically grown from asexually reproduced clones, 1 to 2 plants per square meter, hand-harvested, dried, trimmed and cured.

Resin Rules

Federal law originally defined marihuana in terms of resin content. Resin was mentioned no less than three times in the definition of "marihuana" encoded in the 1970 Controlled Substances Act, which was lifted word-for-word from the 1937 Marihuana Tax Act:

The term "marihuana" means all parts of the plant Cannabis sativa L. [sic], whether growing or not; the seeds thereof; the resin extracted from any part of such plant; and every compound, manufacture, salt, derivative, mixture, or preparation of such plant, its seeds or resin. Such term does not include the mature stalks of such plant, fiber produced from such stalks, oil or cake made from the seeds of such plant, any other compound, manufacture, salt, derivative, mixture, or preparation of such mature stalks (except the resin extracted therefrom), fiber, oil or cake, or the sterilized seed of such plant which is incapable of germination.

In plain English, this says that certain parts of the plant ("mature stalk" and "sterilized seed") are exempt from the legal definition of marijuana. But not included in this exemption are the flowers, the leaves, and the sticky resin wherever it is found on the plant.

Federal law was unequivocal on this point: the resin from any part of the marijuana plant, or any "preparation" made from the resin, is strictly out of bounds. Fiber produced from hemp stalk and oil pressed from hempseed got a legal pass, but not the resin. The Feds didn't want anyone messing with the resin.

As far as medicinal and recreational cannabis goes, the resin is where the action is. The resin contains THC (tetrahydrocannabinol) and CBD (cannabidiol), along with dozens of other secondary plant metabolites (primarily other cannabinoids and terpenoids) that augment human brain chemistry and alleviate physiological and psychological distress.

The sticky, gooey cannabis resin is sequestered within the heads of tiny, mushroom-shaped trichomes, found mainly on the plant's odiferous female flowers (the buds) and to a lesser extent on the leaves. There are also the measly sessile trichomes, which dot the stalk of the hemp plant, but these contain hardly any resin. Non-glandular hairs shaped like tiny inverted commas also cover the plant's surface.

Report Advertisement

Among low resin hemp varietals, dioecious oilseed plants (for making nutritional oil, body care and industrial products) have a higher density of trichomes than monoecious fiber hemp plants. Hempseed oil is not the same as CBD-rich oil extracted from the flowers and leaves of the plant. Oil pressed from hempseed contains no CBD, no THC, no plant cannabinoids to speak of, but it's excellent for making varnish, paint, soap, nutraceuticals, and much more.

The THC Trap

Right from the start, the Feds assumed that resin content was the key factor that distinguished marijuana from industrial hemp. Today, however, federal law includes a recently added caveat that officially characterizes industrial hemp as having no more than 0.3 percent THC by dry weight. Such a tiny amount of THC would not have a euphoric (or dysphoric) effect.

Where did the 0.3 percent THC figure come from? It stems from a 1976 taxonomic report by Canadian plant scientists Ernest Small and Arthur

Cronquist, who never intended for 0.3 percent THC to function as a legal demarcation between hemp and other forms of cannabis.

The Drug Enforcement Administration opened this can of worms when it tried to ban hemp food products, including nutrient-dense hempseed oil, even though these products are about as psychoactive as a baked potato. On October 9, 2001, the DEA published an "Interpretative Rule," which stated that "any product that contains any amount of THC is a schedule I controlled substance."

But this ungainly attempt to destroy hemp food commerce in America would falter thanks to the efforts of the Hemp Industries Association (HIA), which engaged in protracted litigation against the DEA. The HIA scored a major victory in February 2004 when the Ninth Circuit Court of Appeals rejected the DEA's hemp food ban on substantive grounds.

The legal status of CBD was not affected by this court decision. The Controlled Substances Act remained the law of the land. Yet CBD hemp oil purveyors would often cite the Feb 2004 court ruling as the basis for asserting that their products are "legal in all 50 states." This court decision, however, never mentions CBD, and the HIA and Joe Sandler, the HIA's lead attorney in the case, maintain that this ruling did not legalize CBD.

The Farm Bill

Nor did the 2004 court decision (HIA, et al. v DEA, et al.) mention a specific percentage of THC as a determinative factor regarding what's permissible in industrial hemp. It wasn't until ten years later with the passage of the Federal Farm Bill, otherwise known as the Agricultural Act of 2014, that the '0.3 percent THC or less' qualification for hemp was enshrined into federal law.

Section 7606 of the Agricultural Act defined "industrial hemp" for the first time in U.S. history and distinguished it from marijuana. Cannabis was hemp, not marijuana, as long as no part of the plant (including the leaves and flowers) exceeded a THC concentration of "more than 0.3 percent on a dry weight basis."

Resin was not mentioned in Section 7606 of the Farm Bill, which also carved out a legal exception for growing industrial hemp in the United States under the auspices of state-approved pilot research programs. This loophole opened up huge opportunities for industrial hemp advocates and entrepreneurs.

Whereas previously only products made from hemp grown abroad could be marketed in the United States, for the first time in many years American farmers were allowed to cultivate industrial hemp on domestic soil, albeit on a provisional basis. But only states that legalized industrial hemp farming could opt into this federally sanctioned agricultural experiment. Growing industrial hemp outside the parameters of state-sanctioned pilot research is still forbidden under federal law.

Bluegrass CBD

Kentucky, an early 19th century hemp-growing bastion, was the first state to launch a multifaceted, federally approved pilot program to study the feasibility of farming fiber hemp and hemp for seed oil, as well as farming

CBD-rich plants for medicinal oil extraction. It is currently legal under state and federal law for certain licensed

Kentuckians to breed, cultivate, and harvest industrial hemp, formulate products, including CBD-rich oil concentrates, and ship these products across state lines.

Because Kentucky chose to operate within the context of a federally sanctioned agricultural program, local hemp farmers could access certified, pedigree seed stock from official European and Canadian sources after obtaining a Controlled Substances Import & Export Permit from the DEA. A pedigree seed supply is crucial to maintain the uniformity and consistency of a large-scale, machine-harvested crop. Today there are hundreds of cultivars available to meet the global demands for many industrial hemp products.

But industrial hemp varieties are not optimal for extracting CBD-rich oil. So Kentucky farmers sought out high-resin, CBD-rich drug plants from sources in states where cannabis is legal for therapeutic use. Bluegrass ambassadors visited CBD-rich clone repositories in Northern California and returned to Kentucky with cuttings of high-resin cannabis strains, including "ACDC," which tips the scales at twenty percent CBD and roughly one percent THC by dry weight. By comparison, some oilseed hemp varieties weigh in at about 3.5 percent CBD max with hardly any THC, while low resin fiber hemp has even less CBD.

ACDC is the prototypical high-resin, non-euphoric, drug-type cannabis plant. It's an excellent source of CBD-rich oil, far more prodigious than any internationally certified industrial hemp cultivar or hemp/marijuana hybrid. But ACDC does not legally qualify as industrial hemp because it slightly exceeds 0.3 percent THC by dry weight.

Colorado Cowboys

ACDC and a number of other high-CBD/low-THC cannabis strains are also being grown in Colorado under the guise of that state's putative industrial hemp program. But Colorado's fledgling hemp industry is not compliant with Section 7606 of the Agricultural Act of 2014.

Instead of growing hemp for research purposes as part of a federally sanctioned pilot initiative, Colorado leapfrogged official protocol and went straight to large-scale commercial cultivation. Thus, while it's legal under state law to grow industrial hemp, make hemp products, and distribute these products within Colorado, federal law prohibits the cross-border transport and sale of Colorado hemp oil products. CBD is not legal in all 50 states, but that hasn't stopped several Colorado start-ups (and others) from marketing CBD-rich "hemp" oil to all 50 states and beyond.

Some farmers in Colorado are actually growing high-resin, CBD-rich drug plants and calling it hemp. These "hemp" growers typically harvest their crop several weeks before maturity (i.e., before peak resin content) to keep the THC level at 0.3 percent or less. But sometimes it doesn't work out that way.

Last year, Ryan Loflin, a Colorado farmer, was forced to destroy his entire crop because it tested at 0.5 percent THC, a smidgen over the arbitrary legal limit. This tragicomic episode underscores the folly of defining hemp, as distinct from marijuana, according to a precise THC percentage.

Whether ACDC or any other high-resin, non-euphoric, CBD-rich cannabis strain measures slightly above or slightly below the 0.3 percent THC limit won't make any appreciable difference in terms of the quality of the CBD-rich oil extract or its therapeutic impact.

Industrial Hemp Revival

Joy Beckerman, president of Hemp Ace International, a Seattle-based consulting firm, teaches a class for law students on "The Curious Legal Status of CBD and Industrial Hemp-Derived Cannabinoids." An industrial hemp entrepreneur and advocate for the past 25 years, Beckerman recognizes that cannabidiol has played a key role in jump-starting the creation of new infrastructure for hemp's vast oilseed and fiber industries.

Simply put, huge interest in CBD's medicinal potential is the main reason why industrial hemp is growing again in the United States.

"I see the revenue that can be immediately generated by the hemp CBD market as leading to the funding of an extensive domestic infrastructure for processing hemp fiber and seed into tens of thousands of natural and manufactured products, as well as CBD oil," says Beckerman.

Project CBD applauds the fact that cannabidiol has helped to liberate industrial hemp from the confines of the drug abuse paradigm.

Catalyzed by CBD, today's industrial hemp revival in the United States is a major step forward that bodes well ecologically and economically. But it also highlights ongoing problems related to cannabis prohibition.

CBD has undoubtedly helped to loosen federal law with respect to industrial hemp. But current federal law prohibits American farmers from growing high-resin CBD-rich drug plants that narrowly exceed the 0.3 percent THC limit, even though these high-resin cannabis plants are much better suited for extracting CBD-rich oil than low-resin industrial hemp. Cannabis oil should be safely extracted without using toxic solvents and it should be formulated into high quality products with no artificial ingredients, chemical preservatives, poisonous thinning agents, or corn syrup.

If a large CBD-rich oil yield is the goal, then it makes little sense to decide whether a plant qualifies as a worthy source of CBD on the basis of THC content. To be clear: The best source of whole plant, CBD-rich oil is high-resin, CBD-rich cannabis—regardless of minor THC variations—that is sustainably grown without the use of pesticides or plant growth regulators. Bottom-line economics, however, may argue in favor of massive acres of seed-germinated, machine-harvested industrial hemp with 3.5 percent CBD, rather than a much smaller number of high resin cannabis plants, grown from clones, with 20 percent CBD by dry weight. Unlike with medicinal cannabis gardens, there are no plant limits for industrial hemp.

For many hemp farmers around the world, CBD oil is actually a co-product or byproduct of industrial hemp grown primarily for another purpose. Farmers can make additional money if they sell their unused hemp biomass to a business that wants to extract CBD from the leftovers. This 'dual-use' practice is widespread among large-scale hemp growers in Canada, for example, but it's technically illegal, entirely unregulated, and the hemp biomass sold via underground channels is often tainted with pesticides and requires toxic solvents to extract the CBD.

Hemp Oil Issues

If grown outdoors in tested soil and carefully processed, industrial hemp can be a viable source of CBD. But it is not an optimal source of CBD-rich oil for several reasons. Industrial hemp typically contains far less cannabidiol than high-resin, CBD-rich cannabis, and huge amounts of skimpy hemp foliage are required to extract a small amount of CBD. This raises the risk of contaminants as hemp is a bio-accumulator, meaning the plant draws toxins from the soil. That's an excellent property for phyto-remedial purposes, but it's not so great for making ingestible medicinal oil concentrates.

Heavily refined CBD paste derived from industrial hemp foliage is poor starter material for formulating CBD-rich oil products.

Both the imported hemp paste and the products infused with "pure" hemp-derived CBD powder that proliferate online typically include a thinning agent, which dilutes the oil that is heated and inhaled by vape pen users. Medical patients should beware of vape pen oil that contains propylene glycol as a thinning agent. When overheated, this chemical additive produces formaldehyde, a carcinogen, as a byproduct, according to a 2015 report in the New England Journal of Medicine. Why do so many vape oil products contain this thinning agent? It's because of the dubious quality of the extracted material from which these unregulated vape oil products are made.

Products with heavily processed "pure" CBD derived from industrial hemp lack the full spectrum of aromatic terpenes and other cannabinoids found in high-resin drug plants. These compounds interact synergistically with CBD and THC to enhance their therapeutic effects. Scientific research shows that whole plant CBD-rich cannabis oil has a broader range of therapeutic attributes and greater therapeutic efficacy than single-molecule CBD.

As far as current federal law goes, any CBD-rich plant that exceeds 0.3 percent THC is considered marijuana and is therefore off limits for growing and extracting. But the Feds are much more lenient when it comes to pharmaceutical THC.

Single-molecule THC (sold as "Marinol") is a Schedule III drug available by prescription in all 50 states, even though it makes one as high as a kite. Schedule III is reserved for therapeutic substances with low abuse potential. Whole plant cannabis, meanwhile, continues to be classified as a dangerous Schedule I drug with no medical value.

Single-molecule compounds are the preferred domain of Big Pharma, which favors patentable isolates over "crude" whole plant synergies. It's only a matter of time before the Food and Drug Administration gives a thumbs-up to synthetic, single-molecule, pharmaceutical CBD. The FDA, however, is generally not in the business of approving plants as medicines (though there are a few exceptions).

The FDA's single-molecule tilt reflects a cultural and political bias that privileges corporate pharmaceuticals.

Single-molecule medicine is the predominant corporate way, the Big Pharma way, but it's not the only way, and there's scant evidence that it's the best way to benefit from cannabis therapeutics.

The FDA Chimes In On February 4, 2016, the FDA issued warning letters to eight CBD hemp oil retailers for making unproven medical claims about 22 different hemp-derived CBD products. The FDA also tested these products for CBD content and found some that contained no cannabidiol. This was the second round of FDA warning letters sent to CBD hemp oil businesses for product mislabeling.

Some of the same products that had been previously identified as containing no CBD were still being hawked by unscrupulous internet storefronts.

Exposing fraud is necessary and laudable on the part of the FDA. That's what a regulatory agency should do to protect vulnerable consumers. Over the years, however, the FDA has undermined its own credibility by marching in lockstep to the drug war drumbeat. On April 20, 2006, for example, the FDA dissed medical marijuana by issuing an advisory memo, which repeated the official fiction that cannabis is both dangerous and therapeutically useless.

Under the current regulatory regime, a product can't be marketed as a medicine unless the FDA approves it as safe and effective for a specific condition. But FDA approval is no guarantee of safety or efficacy.

Big Pharma, like Big Tobacco, routinely falsifies studies by hiding clinical trial data about adverse side effects and negative outcomes. And all too often, the FDA handles corporate criminals with kid gloves.

Limited by single-molecule dogma and allergic to plant compounds that can't be patented, Big Pharma is way behind the curve with respect to cannabis therapeutics. For all its billions, Big Pharma hasn't done much for children with intractable epilepsy. Little Charlotte Figi in Colorado, featured on CNN, wasn't helped by Big Pharma. It was oil from a resinous CBD-rich cannabis plant that stopped her chronic seizures and saved her life.

The Seven Percent Solution

Charlotte's Web, the CBD-rich strain that does wonders for children with Dravet's Syndrome, isn't a FDA-approved pharmaceutical. It came from marijuana growers in Colorado, where medicinal cannabis is legal. A lab analysis of Charlotte's Web from ROC [Realm of Caring] Labs, dated October 16, 2013, reports the total CBD content at 7.28 percent and THC at 0.24 percent.

These numbers suggest that Charlotte's Web might be a cross between high-resin cannabis and industrial hemp. For marketing purposes, however, Charlotte's Web was promoted as hemp and nothing but hemp.

Rumors abound regarding the origins of this strain. Its CBD content is about the same as CBD levels in certain offshoots of 'Finola,' a leading industrial hemp cultivar bred for nutritional seed protein and seed oil by Jace Callaway, an American medical chemist who lives in Finland. "We reliably measured CBD in 'Finola' samples up to eight percent in open pollinated field conditions (individual plants), but the field average is just between 3-4 percent," Callaway told Project CBD, adding: "'Finola' typically has a 1:15 ratio of THC to CBD. Some individual plants can be isolated and cloned from 'Finola' with much higher ratios . . . These are now all over the place." GW Pharmaceuticals, a British firm at the forefront of developing cannabis-based medications, utilizes a proprietary cultivar known as 'Grace,' which measures around seven percent cannabidiol and sub-0.3 percent THC. 'Grace' is grown outdoors in the United Kingdom.

Bucking the Big Pharma trend while establishing a foothold in that sphere, GW is researching whole plant CBD-THC combinations, as well as cannabis-derived isolates.

Seven percent CBD is not nearly as attractive as twenty percent CBD (the California standard) if the goal is to grow and harvest cannabis for maximum CBD-rich oil production. European and North American botanists, accordingly, have set their sights on breeding a stable politically correct seed line with a CBD level that tops the charts and barely any THC so that it technically qualifies as industrial hemp under federal law.

The Straight Dope

When it comes to CBD-rich oil production, the 0.3 percent THC legal limit is an absurd, impractical, resin-phobic relic of reefer madness. It has become the lynchpin of cannabis prohibition, a venal, dishonest policy that impedes medical research and blocks patient access to valuable therapeutic options, including herbal extracts with various CBD:THC ratios. For patients struggling with a wide range of conditions, CBD and THC work best together, enhancing each other's beneficial effects.

Thus far, twenty-three U.S. states have enacted medical marijuana laws and 17 states have passed versions of 'CBD-only' laws that ostensibly permit the therapeutic use of high CBD/low THC products.

None of the 'CBD-only' states, except for Kentucky, are in compliance with federal law regarding industrial hemp.

There's no consensus as to the proper THC limit for industrial hemp: North Carolina puts it at 0.9 percent; in Texas, it's 0.5 percent. Each state government sets its own dysfunctional rules. Some states limit the sources of CBD-rich products and specify a narrow range of conditions for which CBD can be used; others do not.

Leading advocates for 'CBD-only' laws have argued that this legislation is a crucial first step toward full-fledged legalization of medical marijuana. Thus far, however, there have been no such advances in any states that passed 'CBD-only' laws. Most patients are not well served by 'CBD-only' laws.

They need access to a wide spectrum of whole plant cannabis remedies, not just low THC products. Confucius once said that to change society one must start by calling things by their real names. If maximizing CBD-rich oil output for product formulation is the objective and the best plant sources are federally illegal because of a minuscule amount of THC, then perhaps it's time to call things by their real name. It's not industrial hemp that's growing when American farmers harvest their cannabis crops before full maturity to minimize THC content. These are high-resin, CBD-rich drug plants, albeit the non-euphoric kind—in essence, marijuana that doesn't make you feel high. And marijuana is still prohibited under federal law.

SOURCING CBD

1. Huge interest in the medicinal potential of CBD has catalyzed a rebirth of industrial hemp in the United States.

2. There are two types of cannabis plants, broadly speaking -- low resin hemp plants and high resin drug plants. Low-resin industrial hemp includes plants grown for fiber and for seed oil. High resin drug plants include euphoric THC-rich plants and non-euphoric CBD-rich plants.

3. Industrial hemp is not an optimal source of CBD-rich oil.

4. Federal law prohibits American farmers from growing high-resin CBD-rich drug plants that narrowly exceed 0.3 percent THC, even though these high-resin cannabis plants are much better suited for extracting CBD-rich oil than low-resin industrial hemp.

5. The 0.3 percent THC federal legal limit for industrial hemp is an aribtrary, impractical, scientifically baseless distinction designed to maintain marijuana prohibition, a disreputable policy built on a mountain of lies.

6. American farmers in Colorado and elsewhere are growing high resin CBD-rich marijuana and calling it hemp. These "hemp" growers typically harvest their crop early to minimize THC content.

7. Colorado start-ups are marketing CBD-rich oil to all 50 states, despite the fact that federal law bans the cross-border transport and sale of Colorado cannabis oil products. CBD is not legal in all 50 states.

8. The Federal Farm Bill of 2014 carved out an exemption for growing and marketing industrial hemp under the auspices of state-approved pilot research programs, but only one state thus far implemented such a program. Licensed farmers in Kentucky are currently allowed to breed, cultivate, and harvest industrial hemp, formulate products, including CBD-rich oil concentrates, and ship these products across state lines.

9. For many hemp farmers in Canada and Europe, CBD oil extraction is actually a co-product or byproduct of industrial hemp grown primarily for another purpose. Farmers earn extra money by illegally selling their leftover hemp biomass to businesses that want to extract CBD.

10. CBD and THC enhance each other's therapeutic effects. Most medical patients need access to a wide spectrum of whole plant cannabis remedies, not just low THC products.

CBD/THC COMPARISON

Even though CBD is the second main substance found in cannabis alongside THC, the two cannot differ more. Let's compare these two with the intention of getting more familiar with CBD, its effects, and status.

First of all, CBD is not psychoactive like THC is. This means that using, let's say hemp oil, will not get you in the state known as 'high', so there are no hallucinatory effects or euphoria. This makes CBD the perfect medicine suitable for younger children as well.

Secondly, CBD is a legal substance worldwide but only when extracted from the hemp plant, since it has a very low amount of THC and the extracted oil does not alter your sensations and perceptions.

Thirdly, as opposed to THC, CBD does not have the effect of making you sleepy, so it won't make you feel dozy or affect your alertness when using it during the day.

Lastly, and most importantly, CBD has no addictive effects. In fact, according to some recent studies, CBD can help in overcoming nicotine addiction. This is one more reason why this supplement is so appealing as a medicine, as there are no studies which show undesirable effects of this cannabinoid yet.

CHAPTER 3

BENEFITS AND EFFECTS OF CBD HEMP OIL

CBD is the ingredient accountable for these plants' positive effects and is highly beneficial in reducing nausea and vomiting, suppressing seizures, combating anxiety, depression, psychosis disorders, inflammatory disorders, neurodegenerative disorders, tumors and cancer cells. Many studies and human trials are yet to be done, but from the ones completed so far and from many individual examples (like the one about Charlotte Figi and her successful treatment of a very rare form of epilepsy), CBD can be used for treating the following medical conditions:

- Chronic pain
- ADD and ADHD
- Addiction
- Anxiety
- Asthma
- Autism
- Cancer
- Digestive issues

- Depression

- Diabetes
- Epilepsy and seizures
- Inflammation
- Kidney and liver disease
- Migraine
- Nausea
- PTSD
- Schizophrenia
- Skin conditions
- Sleep conditions
- Stress

Inhibition of adenosine uptake leads to increased adenosine signaling, which may explain the ability of CBD to decrease inflammation and to present neuroprotective effects . Another similar mechanism has also been reported for CBD, according to which this cannabinoid could block anandamide uptake and inhibit its enzymatic hydrolysis .

Few studies have been completed concerning the safety and side effects of CBD after its administration in vivo and in vitro, but this review will summarize such findings.

First, CBD safety in animals and humans will be discussed. Second, side effects of CBD intake will be discussed, as well as the biological parameters affected by CBD interaction with other substances. Finally, some toxicology aspect studied in monkey will be shown.

METHOD

This review was conducted using reports retrieved from Web of Science, Scielo and Medline

The reference lists of eligible papers were checked for additional relevant studies. Studies describing mixed cannabinoids or CBD extracts were excluded. A total of papers were selected for the review.

RESULTS

Safety of CBD Effect on Cell Growth and Embryogenesis CBD exerts anti-proliferative and pro-apoptotic effects in tumor cell lines. There are several mechanisms by which CBD exhibits its effects, including the production of reactive oxygen species (ROS) and concomitant activation of initiator caspase-8 and caspase, inhibition of the procarcinogenic lipoxygenase pathway, and induction of apoptosis, inhibition of tumor grown.

In order to investigate the selectivity of CBD's effects in tumoral and nontumoral cells, several concentrations of CBD were tested in vitro on different stabilized nontumor cell lines, such as human keratinocyte, rat preadipocytes, and mouse monocytemacrophages.

CBD does not affect the vitality of non-tumor cell lines, contrary to what occurs with human breast carcinoma cells, human prostate carcinoma cells, human colorectal carcinoma cells, human gastric adenocarcinoma cells, rat glioma cells, rat thyroid cells transformed with the v-K-ras oncogene, and rat basophilic leukemia cells. Glial cells were also tested against CBD toxicity and their viability was not affected by the treatment with CBD up to 50µM. The safety of CBD on non-transformed cells may be explained by the lack of ROS damage in glial cells.

Analysis of CBD's effects on embryo development is also important, because it raises the question whether expectant mothers can take CBD, and, consequently, whether it affects fetal development. In vitro results revealed that CBD did not significantly alter embryonic development at concentrations of 6.4, 32 and 160 nM.

Effect on Food Intake

One common effect of THC is increased food intake, which is mediated by CB1 and induced by stimulation of dopamine release in the nucleus accumbens.

CBD has a low affinity for the CB1 receptor, and concentrations of 3 to 100 mg/kg body weight (bw) administered intraperitoneally (i.p.) resulted in no significant effects on food intake in mice or rats. However, CBD (20mg/kg bw i.p.) decreased hyperphagia induced by CB1 and 5-HT1A receptor agonists in rats. Conversely, chronic use of CBD for up to 14 days reduced body weight gain in rats at doses of 2.5 and 5 mg/kg bw. This effect was prevented by co-administration of a CB2 receptor antagonist.

Cataleptic Effects and Motor Changes Typical antipsychotic drugs exhibit catalepsy as a side effect, which is mediated by the blockade of dopamine receptors in the dorsal striatum. These drugs may counteract the stereotypical actions of dopaminergic agents in rodents, including d-amphetamine, and hyperlocomotion induced by dopaminergic agents or antagonism of the N-methyl-daspartate (NMDA) glutamate-receptor subtype.

Moreover, these dopaminergic agents cause decreased social interaction and disruption of the prepulse inhibition of the startle reflex. The antagonism of these effects is predictive for compounds with antipsychotic activity. Several studies have evaluated the antipsychotic-like properties of CBD in animal models. This cannabinoid has not been shown to induce catalepsy, even at doses as high as 480 mg/kg bw. Motor changes were investigated in studies of possible anxiolytic and antidepressant effects of CBD. Antidepressant drugs activate the 5-HT1A receptors, and CBD may also exhibit agonist properties at 5-HT1A receptors.

CBD shows anxiolytic-like and antidepressant-like effects with an inverted U-shaped profile, but does not induce motor changes.

Effects on Physiological Parameters in Animals Several studies administering CBD by different routes have shown it to be safe, in regards to the effects on physiological parameters.

At a wide range of doses (3-30mg/kg bw i.p.), CBD does not affect blood pressure, heart rate, body temperature, glucose levels, pH, Pco_2, Po_2, hematocrit, K^+ or Na^+ levels, gastrointestinal transit or rectal temperature in rodents . The results were the same, even after 14 days of treatment.

An in vitro study showed that the cannabinoid failed to induce contraction in mouse small intestine at concentrations ranging from 0.01mol/L to 10.0mol/L. Furthermore, CBD has not shown significant effects on open-field physiological activity (defecation and urination) nor on vocalization behavior.

Mice treated with 60 mg/kg bw CBD i.p. three times per Safety, Side Effects of Cannabidiol Current Drug Safety, 2011, Vol. 6, No. 4 3 week for 12 weeks did not experience significant side effects such as ataxia, kyphosis, generalized tremor, swaying gait, or tail stiffness. Finally, CBD at 10 and 20mg/kg bw i.p. did not produce emesis in mice.

Another study performed to determine whether CBD is an agonist at rat TRPV1 receptors in vivo demonstrated the safety of this cannabinoid in other physiological parameters.

Rats received a CBD injection (0.003-6.36mol; 1-2,000gintra-arterially), but did not exhibit appreciable effects on mean blood pressure, arterial blood gas tensions, pH, ventilatory responses or respiratory minute volume. This study provided evidence that CBD does not affect ventilation.

Stimulation of vanilloid receptors induces vasodilation and inflammation. CBD has been shown to be a full agonist of human TRPV1 at concentrations lower than those needed to bind to CB1/CB2 receptors, usually at doses ranging from 10 to 50 mg/kg in humans, followed by a quick desensitization of TRPV1 receptors, which leads to the depletion of sensory nociceptors.

CBD (0.1-30mg/kg bw intravenously (i.v.)) had no effect on the rate of intestinal transit or the rate of gastric emptying, or cardiovascular, antinociception, hypothermia or respiratory parameters. An evaluation of the neuroprotective activity of CBD revealed that CBD was not only free from significant side effects, but also associated with cardiac, hemodynamic, and ventilatory benefits in piglets.

It is important to note that the lack of CBD side effects was observed during studies whose primary objectives were not to evaluate CBD´s safety, but to study cannabinoid activity.

Furthermore, several other studies that evaluated the anxiolytic effects of CBD in rodents demonstrated the safety and tolerability of this drug in rodents.

Effects on Monoamine Oxidase Activity

CBD (0.3-300g/mg protein) was ineffective at inhibiting porcine monoamine oxidase activity of brain and liver mitochondria after 1 hr of incubation with mitochondrial preparation.

Effects on Memory

Short-term memory and other cognitive deficits have been reported in humans after smoking marijuana. In rats tested against a delayed match to sample task, THC showed a correlation between delay and dose-dependent behavioral deficit produced in this task. This performance was selectively impaired by a lack of discharge of hippocampal neurons. However, CBD at doses of 0.75-2.0mg/kg bw (i.p.) were tested in the same task and no significant effect on performance was observed [59].

Effects at Estrogen Receptors

Compounds possessing the tricyclic cannabinoid structure, including CBD, have been reported to interact with rodent estrogen receptors.

To test the hypothesis that cannabinoids produce a direct activation of estrogen receptors, Ruh et al. [60] investigated whether cannabinoid compounds exhibit estrogen-induced mitogenesis in MCF-7 breast cancer cells. CBD (1 and 10µM) did not significantly stimulate the proliferative response or transcriptional activity compared to controls. As a result, CBD failed to behave as an estrogen receptor agonist in vitro.

Studies in Humans

In human studies, CBD administration did not induce side effects across a wide range of dosages, including acute and chronic dose regimens, and tolerance to CBD did not develop.

Acute Studies

In the 1970s, human studies showed that oral CBD intake from 15 to 160mg, inhalation of 0.15mg/kg bw or intravenous injection from 5 to 30mg were not followed by ill effects.

CBD does not interfere with several psychomotor and psychological functions in humans. CBD does not affect heart rate, blood pressure, or performance in the verbal paired-associate learning test as measured by recall score at doses up to 600mg.

Subsequent studies concerning the antipsychotic effects of CBD have not reported any side effects after CBD intake.

Chronic Studies

Chronic oral administration of 10mg CBD daily for 21 days did not induce any changes in neurological (including electroencephalogram (EEG)), clinical (including electrocardiogram (EKG)), psychiatric, blood or urine examinations. Likewise, oral CBD administration in healthy participants

(3mg/kg bw daily for 30 days) and in epileptic patients (200-300mg daily for 135 days) was well tolerated and no signs of toxicity or serious side effects were detected on neurological and physical examinations, blood and urine analysis, or EKG and EEG, which were performed at weekly intervals. CBD was evaluated for symptomatic efficacy and safety in 15 neuroleptic-free patients with Huntington's Disease.

Effects after oral CBD (10mg/kg bw /day for 6 weeks) or placebo (sesame oil for 6 weeks) intake were evaluated weekly under a double-blind, randomized crossover design. CBD showed no significant or clinical differences compared to placebo in the Cannabis side effect inventory, clinical lab tests or other safety outcome variables. Also, weekly plasma levels of CBD (mean range 5.9 to 11.2 ng/ml), assayed by GC/MS, did not differ significantly over the 6 weeks of CBD administration.

A previous case report of a teenager diagnosed with schizophrenia who experienced severe side effects after treatment with conventional antipsychotics demonstrated significant improvement of symptoms with no adverse effects after hospitalization and 4 weeks of treatment with increasing doses of CBD up to 1,500mg/day.

More recently, CBD monotherapy was administered to three patients with treatment-resistant schizophrenia (initial oral dose of 40 mg, increased to 1,280mg/day) for up to 4 weeks with no side effects reported, even at the highest dose.

The efficacy and safety of CBD on Parkinson's disease patients with psychotic symptoms were study in a 4-week open trial. A flexible oral dose of CBD, ranging from 150mg/day to 400mg/day in the last week, plus patients' usual treatments showed that psychotic symptoms were significantly reduced; cognitive and motor symptoms were not affected by the cannabinoid and no serious side effects were reported. A double-blind placebo controlled trial is currently underway by our group to evaluate the efficacy, safety, and tolerability of CBD in patients with Parkinson's disease and psychosis.

Finally, a 19-year old female with a history of cannabis addiction received CBD 300mg on day 1, 600mg/day divided into two doses days 2 through 10, and CBD 300mg on day 11. During treatment with CBD, the patient did not report any marijuana withdrawal symptoms, and she did not experience anxiety or dissociative symptoms or improved sleep quality, as assessed by standardized rating scales.

We did not include in this review studies on cannabis extracts or CBD-rich extracts, as the other several compounds may have multiple interactions with CBD.

However, some clinical trials in multiple sclerosis have shown that the 1:1 mix of THC and CBD, which is available as an oromucosal spray (Sativex) at doses ranging from 2.5 to 120 mg of each cannabinoid, showed no adverse effects on cognition or mood or other than those observed with psychoactive drugs for pain treatment.

SIDE EFFECTS OF CBD HEPM OIL

The Known Side Effects of Cannabidiol

What do people need to know about the side effects of cannabidiol before turning to it as a viable treatment? Find out the possible risk factors at Sol CBD.

There are two sides to nearly every modern medicine, both within the traditional and alternative sectors. When a patient takes medication for its positive characteristics which target a specific health issue or ailment, they should also acknowledge that many treatments have unwanted characteristics that go hand-in-hand with their benefits. The side-effects can often lead people to take even more medication to handle them, and still other people choose to seek alternative medicines which typically have less severe or fewer unwanted effects.

This has led many people to turn towards cannabidiol (CBD) as an alternative therapy considering its wide ranging medical benefits but low negative reactions. Does this mean that CBD has no side-effects? What do people need to understand about CBD's possible risk factors prior to turning to it as a viable treatment?

The good news is that the vast majority of research into the subject has found that CBD treatments show little to no risk of side-effects; even in higher doses of up to 1,500 mg a day.

Unlike its sister substance, THC, CBD doesn't have any psychoactive effects, nor does it seem to alter heart rate, appetite, blood pressure or body temperature.

However, with all this in mind there has been some evidence to suggest that it can interact with some pharmaceuticals, and cause decreased activity of p-glycoprotien. Cannabidiol has been proven to interact with cytochrome P450 enzymes, which are located within your liver.

What all this scientific lingo is saying, is that CBD can inhibit or otherwise affect the movement of or absorption of pharmaceuticals within the body, especially in higher doses. Especially in the case of its interactions with your liver enzymes, CBD can affect the way medication is metabolized through the liver. That being said, this is specifically the side-effect being sought after by some people as in one example, CBD will inhibit the negative effects of THC. It is also interesting to note that everyday foods also can have the same effects on the liver, including grapefruit.

Other studies have found that CBD can in some cases increase the sensation of dry-mouth. This is likely caused by the way cannabidiol interacts directly with the endocannabinoid system, specifically CB-1 and CB-2 receptors. These receptors are present within the glands responsible for saliva production, and CBD can therefore alter saliva production and cause the sensation of dry-mouth.

In still another study, increased tremors and muscular movements were recorded for Parkinson's patients on extremely high doses of CBD.

Strangely enough CBD treatment has been shown to be extremely effective for many people suffering from Parkinson's Disease and therefore the negative responses may be associated with a specific dosage. In past studies of CBD's effect on animals, where monkeys were given extremely high doses of CBD, tremors and cardiac failure were recorded. Those animals who were subsequently given lower doses, recovered completely within a few days.

These studies have never been replicated in humans, and as noted before, CBD has never shown any strongly adverse reactions even in higher doses (up to 1500mg a day in one often cited study) for humans. Obviously more research in this area is needed to better understand the nuances of CBD's dosage and its effect on Parkinson's and other health issues.

The inhibitory effect that CBD treatment has on the human immune system is also a double edged sword. In some cases, this may be specifically why someone chooses to use CBD, while in others it can be considered a true side effect. For instance, the specific manner in which CBD inhibits the human immune system also may increase some disease progression, HIV-infection, as well as metastasization of tumors. In this case though, there is also a suggestion that it is the dosage which alters the effect on the body, as lower doses do not tend to show these same effects.

In animal studies, high CBD doses have affected fertilization capacity. This has yet to be demonstrated in a human clinical trial, but at least in the study of sea-urchins it has been found to reduce the fertilization capacity of sperm.

For women who are pregnant or breastfeeding, there is currently little to no research available on the possible side-effects of using CBD.

Therefore, until there is a solid understanding of CBD during these times, it is recommended that pregnant and nursing women avoid using CBD treatments.

The fact that CBD has such low risk of side-effects is exactly why many people are turning towards it has an alternative treatment. Typically, people using CBD as an alternative treatment have already weaned themselves off of most pharmaceuticals and therefore CBD will have no negative interactions. Finally, the few side-effects which have been recorded are limited and rare; typically, only present with higher dosages.

Effect of Cannabidiol in the Human Immune System

The majority of available literature shows inhibitory capacities of cannabinoids, including CBD, on cells of the human immune system.

CBD (2.5-10g/ml) strongly inhibited interleukin (IL)-10 production in a virus-negative T-cell line, and increased IL-8, macrophage inflammatory protein 1 (MIP-1) and MIP-1 production in an eosinophilic leukemia cell line and inhibited IL-8 production by B-cells.

Since CBD decreased production of IL-8 and CC chemokines (MIP-1 and MIP-1) by B-cells, a patient's risk of infection with human immunodeficiency virus – 1 (HIV-1) or other infectious organisms may increase, along with a risk of disease progression. Previous reports suggested that IL-10 inhibits HIV-1 expression by infected macrophages.

Therefore, the strong inhibition of IL-10 production by CBD could be another mechanism by which this cannabinoid can up regulate HIV-1 production. In summary, although these effects are of potential benefit in some conditions, they may worsen disease progression, HIV infection, tumor genesis, and metastases, and exacerbate allergic inflammation in the lung.

However, some results suggested that CBD could yield a biphasic response in the immune system with stimulatory capacity at lower doses (nanomolar concentrations) and inhibitory activity at higher doses (micromolar concentrations).

Accordingly, an enhancement of mitogeninduced indoleamine 2,3-dioxygenase activity and secretion of interferon (IFN) by CBD (10-

100ng/ml) and suppression of these activities at higher doses (1-10µg/ml) were observed in human peripheral blood mononuclear cells.

CHAPTER 4

CBD HEPM OIL BUYER'S GUIDE

Now that more and more states are passing bills to legalize CBD products and people are starting to learn about the benefits and uses of CBD oil, the market for hemp-derived products is expected to increase even more.

While it's surely a good thing to make CBD oil easily available for people all over the world, the increasing popularity of products rich in cannabinoids has a not so pleasant side effect. Driven by the desire to explore this business opportunity and get the most of it, producers use misleading marketing and deceptive advertising to increase profits.

In order to convince people to buy CBD oil or other products made of hemp or containing cannabidiol, companies claim that their CBD can cure pretty much anything from cancer to acne scars, yet they have no scientific argument to back up their statements. It's therefore not surprising to see that people are reluctant when it comes to purchasing such products, or that they feel overwhelmed and have no idea how to buy CBD oil without getting scammed.

What sounds more appealing to you? To search for a hemp shop in your area, or to try an online shop that sells hemp oil or other cannabinoid-rich products? Regardless of your choice, the first and most important thing to do before you buy any product that contains cannabidiol is to do your homework and make sure you know what you're getting.

CBD HEMP OIL DIFFEFERNT PRODUCTS

Most of the CBD that you would use medicinally is found in the least processed form of the cannabis plant, which is hemp. Hemp and marijuana come from the same plant, but because of breeding, they are drastically different. Growers who produce marijuana have bred it selectively to alter different things such as smell, the concentration of THC, and the like. Hemp, though, hasn't been bred that way, so it is the purest form of the plant, and it is where CBD oil comes from.

Cbd Oil Cream:

When you use CBD oil in a cream form, you're essentially using a lotion infused with the oil. These are applied transdermally to the area that you're trying to target. These creams are used for things like pain, inflammation, or general soreness in a particular area of the body.

CBD oil cream is a great option for sports related injuries. There is also some evidence of this application helping with dermatitis, headaches, itching, and more. The CBD in this cream delivery method doesn't penetrate down into the bloodstream. Instead, it reacts with the body's CB2 receptors. CBD oil creams are sometimes prepared with mint, or cayenne, to target specific symptoms.

HOW IT WORKS

Endocannabinoids are natural signals in your body that help maintain homeostasis by detecting and regulating hunger, pain, mood, and memory.

CBD helps elevate your natural levels of pain-relieving endocannabinoids by blocking metabolism as they're moving around your body.

The second method of pain relief centers around the damage you do when you work out. When you strength train, you create micro-tears in your muscles, which is why you feel sore as you heal. Once your immune cells detect damage, they release inflammatory mediators in order to repair the tissue. CBD, though has the ability to limit the release of some proinflammatory signals, thereby helping with pain without thwarting the healing entirely.

Finally, you have receptors called TrpV1 that detect and regulate your body temperature. When activated, they put out heat, soothing your pain receptors. Using this channel, CBD makes these pain receptors hyperactive for a period of time, causing them to get hot, desensitizing them and downregulating those pain-sensing nerve endings.

CBD Oil Tinctures

Tinctures are the most popular form of CBD oil, which means there many options available. This tincture stands above the rest due to its high-quality ingredients, effectiveness and ease of use.

The spray functionality makes taking this CBD oil a snap. Just two sprays under your tongue, wait 90 seconds, and swallow, and you should feel the effects in less than 10 minutes. The Herbal Renewals CBD Spray comes in three great flavors: Vanilla, Peppermint, and Unflavored (for those who prefer the natural taste of CBD with its earthy, hempy undertones).

Tincture offers a lower concentration of the compound; this is most commonly used for depression and to help with anxiety and insomnia.

HOW IT WORKS

Step 1

Shake well!

Separation in hemp oil products is completely natural and to be expected. Some bottles are impossible to see into (which is good — dark bottles help block light for optimal shelf life), but if you can, take note of how the oil tends to settle onto the bottom. Once you start shaking, it quickly blends.

I can't stress how important this step is. If you don't shake it, you'll likely end up consuming straight grape seed and coconut oil. It's not the tastiest experience, and won't be very beneficial for you either.

Step 2

Squeeze the dropper top to fill the pipette with oil and dispense the oil under your tongue. You can swish it around a little, but most people like to just let it sit (that way you avoid some of the hemp taste — albeit Tasty Drops actually tastes great if you choose a flavored version). You can add as many droppers full as needed; don't feel you need to restrict yourself to the recommended serving size.

The phytocannabinoids in our proprietary blend are non-psychoactive. However, many people have noted a slight sedative effect at larger quantities. This may be beneficial if you have trouble sleeping, so consider using it before bed.

Allow the oil to absorb into your system by holding the oil in your mouth for 60-90 seconds before swallowing. You may choose to swish it around, but it's not necessary. If you find the flavor to be too strong, take a drink of juice as you ingest the oil to mask that hempy flavor (apple cider works very well).

Step 3

Repeat as necessary throughout the day. As mentioned above, hemp oil may be slightly sedative at higher amounts, or simply calming and relaxing at a lower serving size.

Vaping CBD Oil

Vaping CBD oil is growing in popularity because of the increased bioavailability seen with this method of consumption.

During vaporization, CBD enters your lungs and diffuses directly into your bloodstream instead of passing through your gut and liver. The first-pass effect is most attributed to the gut wall and the liver, and that is when fractions of the drug are lost before reaching systemic circulation.

When you vape CBD oil, you don't have to worry about that, which means that more of the CBD can get into your system and faster.

This is why vaping CBD oil is great for anxiety, and nausea, as these are things you would want to dissipate quickly. Also, because you will feel more effects and faster, this allows less CBD to be used at one time.

HOW IT WORKS

There are several different devices for vaporizing cannabis oil, but the most common is the vape pen. It's a simple, disposable device that can be used with simple, disposable cannabis oil cartridges. The pen component recharges via USB (or plugs into a wall with a USB adapter), and charges often last for at least one day.

Due to the universality of cannabis oil cartridges, they can be plugged in to most tobacco vaporizers — if you want to use your own rig for whatever reason, you likely can.

In the case of the standard vape pen, there is no concept of "on" or "off." You simply pull from the mouthpiece of the pen and it lights up, slightly heating the oil and enabling you to inhale cannabis oil vapor.

CBD Oil Gum and Candy

You can also find gum, or even candy, that contains CBD oil. The first product of this kind is gum that was created by "internationally renowned medical doctors, dental and OR surgeons in combination with a well-experienced product development team." It is called CanChew. This product is for treating a range of symptoms like anxiety, pain, nausea, and vomiting.

Chewing gum is a highly effective way to medicate because the CBD will come in direct contact with the mucosal membranes in your mouth and be quickly absorbed into the body.

CBD Oil Capsules

Some people boast that taking CBD oil in capsule form is safer, and it is possible. The main safety benefit is that capsules offer pre-measured doses, so for an older patient or someone who may struggle with dosing, this is an awesome alternative.

The big advantage of CBD oil capsules the convenience of it. You can just take one to two capsules a day for pain management, stress relief, anxiety – anything you would need to take CBD for. The capsule is a fast delivery method and is a good choice if you do not like the taste of CBD oil.

CBD Oil Patches

CBD oil patches are another topical method, but with the patch, the cannabinoids would be able to penetrate into the bloodstream.

A patch is a medicated adhesive that is placed on the skin to deliver a specific dose of medication – through the skin and into the bloodstream, promoting healing to an injured area of the body.

An advantage of transdermal drug delivery over other delivery systems like oral, intravenous, intramuscular, etc. is that a patch provides a controlled release of the drug. It's done through a porous membrane or through body heat that melts medication formulations embedded in the adhesive and allows it to be absorbed.

Concentrates

CBD concentrates typically contain the strongest dosage of CBD compared to any other CBD products. It can contain up to 10 times the average CBD products. Concentrates are also convenient in that it only takes a few seconds to consume.

How to Use

Similar to tinctures, Place the concentrate under your tongue and along the cheeks and ingest it slowly. Overall, CBD concentrates seem to be most popular among customers who are extremely busy, yet seek high potency CBD.

Sprays

CBD sprays are typically the weakest in concentration among the different type of CBD products. Typical concentration of CBD sprays ranges from 1-3mg.

How to Use

Spray one serving of the bottle into your mouth. Serving size should be labeled on the bottle (typically 2-3 sprays). Use daily or as needed.

HOW TO BUY CBD OIL – WATCH OUT FOR THESE 3 TRAPS!

1. Look for quality, not for low prices.

With so many products only one click away, it's more than tempting to grab the most affordable CBD oil you can find online, but cheaper isn't necessarily better. If you Google "buy CBD oil" right now you'll get more than 5,950,000 results, but you know what's curious? Most of these producers and distributors offer no tangible evidence to support the claim that their products are the best. Surely, lower prices are more attractive, but if I were you, I would think twice before picking the cheap CBD oil over the high quality one.

If you want to make sure you're getting a safe and effective product, look for quality, not for a low price. How is quality defined when it comes to CBD oil? The higher the concentration of cannabidiol in a product, the more powerful its effects, and thus the wiser the investment.

2. Beware of products that claim to cure everything.

If you decide to order CBD oil online, start by learning about the real properties and benefits of cannabinoids. Hemp seed oil and Hemp CBD oil are two different products, and neither of them is "medical marijuana".

You'll hear and read a lot about CBD products that can cure different forms of cancer and about hemp oil that has miraculously healed patients from anxiety, tumors, diabetes and whatnot. My advice? Beware of products whose benefits sound too good to be true. CBD hemp oil is a powerful antioxidant whose strength is greater than that of vitamin C and E, and I'm sure we will soon have strong medical evidence for different health effects.

However, at this point, research is still needed, and the surest way to avoid scams is to beware of those products that claim to cure everything. Maybe they do have beneficial properties, but playing with people's minds and hearts and with their desperate need to find a reliable treatment for painful conditions is not the right way to promote a product.

It is a product that is safe and is obtained through a technology that allows it to retain all the nutrients found in the original plant. It's the synergistic action of these nutrients that make CBD oil so valuable and beneficial for one's overall health. We therefore encourage you to add this nutritional supplement to your diet in order to experience the positive effects of the phytonutrients found in our hemp-derived product.

3. Make sure your oil is Non-Psychoactive.

Some of the hemp and marijuana products available on the market contain psychoactive compounds, however cannabidiol is scientifically proven to be anti-psychoactive, so it's important to check the label before buying a

CBD hemp oil and to choose only products that have no psychoactive effects.

As long as you stick with non-psychoactive products there's no risk of getting high from them. But again, beware of cheap products. Making a good CBD oil that retains only the beneficial compounds from hemp requires a certain technology, and that technology is costly.

Few days ago I came across this article saying that you can make CBD oil at home by smashing some hemp seeds and extracting that fluid. Let me tell you something – this way you will get (at best!) a poorly qualitative hemp oil. You can't take the psychoactive THC out of cannabis oil by simply squeezing the liquid from some seeds.

CHAPTER 5

CBD HEP OIL PHARMACOKINETICS

The correct use of CBD in human therapy necessarily requires basic information related to pharmacokinetics.

Cannabis derivatives are usually inhaled or orally administered. Other routes, including rectal, transdermic, eye drops, aerosols and intravenous have been used in a small number of studies so that the relevance of findings is limited. Recently, it was demonstrated in rabbits that sublingual administration of a solid CBD/beta-cyclodextrin complex may provide an alternative formulation for sublingual administration (Mannila et al., 2007). The pharmacokinetics of CBD is quite complicated and in many aspects resembles that of Δ9-THC. Once taken orally, CBD bioavailability ranges between 13% and 19%, due to a marked first-pass effect, while the systemic bioavailability of inhaled CBD in a group of cannabis users was 31% (range 11– 45%). The plasma pattern was similar to that of Δ9-THC. Daily oral doses of CBD 10 mg/kg/day chronically administered resulted in mean plasma concentrations of 5.9–11.2 ng/mL (Consroe et al., 1991a). CBD is rapidly distributed when intravenously administered, and easily passes the blood–brain barrier. CBD shows a prolonged elimination; its terminal halflife is about 9 h, and it is excreted preferentially in the urine, both free and as its glucuronide compound (Samara et al., 1990).

Cannabidiol impairs hepatic drug metabolism in several animal species, and inhibits mouse hepatic metabolism through the inactivation of specific cytochrome P450 belonging to the 2C and 3A subfamilies (Bornheim et al., 1993). The metabolism of CBD showed biotransformation routes typically observed for cannabinoids (Harvey et al., 1991a). It undergoes multiple hydroxylations, oxidations to carboxylic acids, beta-oxidation, conjugation and epoxidation (Harvey et al., 1991a). Conjugation with fatty acids, first observed with Δ9- and Δ8-THC, provides a potent means of increasing the lipophilicity and, hence, tissue accumulation (Leighty et al., 1976). CBD-7-oic acid together with CBD-glucuronide represent the most abundant products of CBD metabolism detected in human urine (Harvey et al.,

1991b). Unlike Δ9-THC a remarkable percentage of unchanged CBD is excreted in the faeces (Wall et al., 1976).

CANCER

Cannabinoids have been studied in the treatment of cancer for some decades. Clinical studies have looked at the reduction of chronic pain, nausea and lack of appetite that resulted from cancer and its treatment. There have also been some molecular and animal studies which show some potential for cannabinoids to kill certain kinds of cancers, although this research is still preliminary.

Pain

There is evidence that the use of cannabinoids reduces chronic pain, whether due to cancer or other causes. A systematic meta-analysis of studies examining the use of cannabinoids for the alleviation of chronic pain from cancer available up to April 2015 conducted by Whiting et al concluded that there was "moderate-quality evidence to support the use of cannabinoids for the treatment of chronic pain".

The review formally assessed study quality, as well as study heterogeneity (agreement between studies on the level of effect), and reviewed over 23,000 documents; in this context, 'moderate-quality' represents an impressive outcome.

Nausea

Dozens of controlled studies were carried out in this area prior to 2001, but despite positive results the area received less research attention after that. Two more recent small controlled studies showed that cannabis-based medicines were more effective than placebo, and were similar in effect to another medicine normally used to counter nausea.

Tumours

Controlled clinical trials on the antitumoral effects of cannabinoids have not been conducted. As a result, there is insufficient evidence to support the use of cannabis treatments in this context. However, according to a leading researcher in this area, Dr Guillermo Velasco, and his colleagues, "It is well-established that cannabinoids exert palliative effects on some cancer-associated symptoms. In addition evidences obtained during the last fifteen years support that these compounds can reduce tumor growth in animal models of cancer. Cannabinoids have been shown to activate an ER-stress related pathway that leads to the stimulation of autophagy-mediated cancer cell death. In addition, cannabinoids inhibit tumor angiogenesis and decrease cancer cell migration."

In 2006, a pilot Phase I clinical trial involving a group of 9 patients with actively growing brain cancer tumours (glioblastoma) who had not responded to standard therapy received intracranial administrations of THC.24 Although the patient group was very small and no control group was used, the results of this study indicated that "some patients responded - at least partially - to THC treatment in terms of decreased tumour growth rate, as evaluated by magnetic resonance imaging". Other research has also identified that the powerful anti-inflammatory capacities of cannabinoids could assist with chronic inflammation associated with new cancer cell growth (neoplasia) and "as a consequence, reducing inflammation as a way of impacting cancer presents a new role for these compounds".

This had led to a new round of research and early phase clinical trials funded by GW Pharmaceuticals to assess the potential of incorporating cannabis medicines into cancer treatment regimes.27 Other significant research projects include the recent announcement from the University of Canberra which will see clinical trials of cannabis treatments for melanoma patients.28 The Lambert Initiative also intends to conduct further cellular and animal testing on the efficacy of certain cannabinoids in the treatment of brain and lung cancers, with a view towards human clinical trials in the future.

It is important to stress that however promising this research might appear, the available evidence in support of using cannabis to treat, prevent or cure cancer is very weak. Using cannabis to treat pain, nausea and appetite in cancer patients is much more strongly supported, as stated by the Cancer Council of NSW and the Clinical Oncology Society of Australia:

"There is no current evidence that cannabis or cannabinoids are effective at inhibiting tumour growth or to treat or cure cancer in humans ... There is some evidence that cannabis and cannabinoids in controlled delivery may have a benefit to cancer patients where conventional treatments are unsuccessful in providing relief in the following areas: for relieving nausea and vomiting in patients undergoing chemotherapy; as an adjunctive analgesic in patients with moderate to severe pain; and/or as an appetite stimulant for patients experiencing weight loss and muscle wasting"

EPILEPSY

Work carried out in the early 1970s demonstrated that CBD possesses a rather potent protective effect against convulsions in a variety of animal models of epilepsy (Carlini et al., 1973; Karler et al., 1973; Karler and Turkanis, 1980; Consroe and Wolkin, 1977a, 1977b). Indeed, some preclinical evidence showed that CBD was remarkably effective against focal seizures, including temporal lobe epilepsy and generalized convulsion induced by both electroshock and GABA receptor blockers. In these experimental paradigms of epilepsy the effects of CBD were considered almost equivalent to those exerted by antiepileptic compounds commonly used in human therapy. Interestingly, CBD was observed to potentiate the anticonvulsant activity of barbiturates and diphenylhydantoin. In this respect it is worth noting that phenytoin and CBD both display similar stereochemical requirements for anticonvulsant drug action (Tamir et al., 1980). Based on these findings, CBD is regarded, among CBs, as the most promising candidate for antiepileptic therapy because of its powerful anticonvulsant properties in the absence of any relevant toxicity. However, besides a great deal of preclinical results, the available literature on CBD use as an anticonvulsant in human therapy is still limited, because it concerns a very few patients.

Many anecdotal reports have confirmed that CBD exerts considerable anticonvulsant activity and the results are efficacious in protecting against partial and tonic-clonic generalized seizures. Indeed, it has been reported that in epileptics who smoked cannabis to control seizures, interrupting cannabis use induced the reappearance of convulsions, whereas reverting to consumption limited symptoms.

Only one double-blind controlled trial was performed to explore the anticonvulsant activity of CBD in 15 patients suffering from frequent attacks of 'secondarily generalized epilepsy' with temporal focus, unresponsive to standard treatment (Cunha et al., 1980). The results of this study indicated that 50% of patients taking CBD remained virtually symptoms-free for the duration of the trial, with no significant toxicity or side effects due to CBD administration. The rest of the patients under medication improved markedly, whereas subjects receiving the placebo remained unchanged. Despite these intriguing results the trial was never continued, in all probability because of the huge amounts of drug required.

Nowadays, CBD treatment has been also proposed as a promising therapeutic tool in monotherapy in children suffering from convulsions, resistant to conventional treatment, even though CBD was found to be ineffective against absence seizures produced in laboratory animals (Cortesi and Fusar-Poli, 2007). This suggestion has been advanced for the absence of tolerance to anticonvulsant properties, also during prolonged treatment with CBD.

This aspect is relevant in subjects who have been treated previously with a high-dose of anticonvulsants or with a combination of them. Moreover, the possibility of administering CBD by metered dose pump aerosol spray guarantees a very useful system of administration in children with a poor compliance.

PSYCHOSIS

Convergent evidence links the habitual use of Cannabis to a risk of developing schizophrenia or schizophrenialike psychosis, especially in vulnerable subjects. This effect has been attributed to Δ9-THC, the main psychoactive constituent of the plant. Conversely, different preclinical studies have provided evidence for a potential antipsychotic activity of CBD, with a pharmacological profile resembling that of a neuroleptic drug.

Indeed, the effects of CBD were similar to those produced by haloperidol in a rodent model predictive of antipsychotic activity, using different doses of drugs (Zuardi et al., 1991). Both CBD and haloperidol reduced the occurrence of apomorphineinduced stereotypies, however, CBD did not provoke catalepsy, even at the highest doses. These results have supported the assumption that CBD possesses antipsychotic properties, without generating extrapyramidal side-effects, thus suggesting the hypothesis that CBD may work as an atypical antipsychotic (Zuardi et al., 1991).

According to this view, the pharmacological profile of CBD was reported to be comparable to that exhibited by clozapine. Interestingly both drugs, in contrast to conventional neuroleptics, induce c-fos expression in mesolimbic and mesocortical structures, but not in basal ganglia (Guimarães et al., 2004).

The first available clinical data, related to this pathology, referred to CBD effects observed in a 19- year-old black woman with schizophrenia (Zuardi et al., 1995).

The administration of CBD resulted in a significant improvement of psychotic symptoms with an efficacy evaluated as equivalent to that of haloperidol.

However, a subsequent clinical study aimed at verifying the efficacy of CBD monotherapy in patients with treatment-resistant schizophrenia (TRS) demonstrated only a mild improvement in one of three patients treated with CBD monotherapy, suggesting that such an approach has to be considered unsatisfactory for TRS (Zuardi et al., 2006). On the other hand, findings have been published reinforcing the suggestions of previous work pointing to the antipsychotic properties of CBD.

Indeed the results have demonstrated that smoking some strains of Cannabis containing more CBD, in addition to Δ9-THC, may be protective against psychotic-like symptoms induced by Δ9-THC alone (Morgan and Curran, 2008).

ANXIETY

The results from several studies performed in the 1980s suggested that CBD displays sedative and antianxiety properties (Pickens, 1981; Musty, 1984; Musty et al., 1984; Zuardi et al., 1982). Such evidence prompted further investigations to be carried out, employing different paradigms, aimed at better defining its intrinsic anxiolytic efficacy. The findings confirmed that CBD exerts significant anxiolytic activity and that antianxiety effects may exhibit an inverted U-shaped dose-response curve in rodents, with the higher doses being no longer effective (Guimaraes et al., 1990, 1994). Moreover, using the elevated plus maze, anxiolytic effects were also reported for the three CBD derivates: HU219, HU252, HU-291 (Guimaraes et al., 1994). The mechanism by which CBD exerts its anxiolytic effects still remains not fully clarified. However, using a conditioned emotional paradigm, the Vogel conflict test, a model of anxiety based on the conflict between drinking and punishment, it was proved that CBD-mediated anxiolytic activity is independent of benzodiazepine receptors or of non-specific drug interference on the nociceptive threshold or water consumption (Moreira et al., 2006).

Recently, the binding at 5HT1A receptor has been considered as a possible molecular target for its antianxiety activity. Indeed, evidence has been provided suggesting that activation of 5HT1A receptors located in the dorsolateral periacqueductal gray could be one of the mechanisms of the anxiolytic effect observed with this compound after systemic administration (Campos and Guimarães, 2008).

In contrast to preclinical studies, few human trials have been conducted to evaluate the efficacy of CBD as an antianxiety agent. Oral administration of CBD in healthy volunteers was found to reduce the anxiogenic effects of Δ9-THC (Zuardi et al., 1982). This property does not seem to implicate pharmacokinetic interactions with Δ9- THC, suggesting that CBD possesses intrinsic anxiolytic properties. Moreover, the anxiolytic effects of CBD were also observed in healthy volunteers submitted to a simulation of a public speaking test. On that occasion CBD (300 mg/per os) exhibited an efficacy comparable to that displayed by diazepam (10 mg/per os) and ipsapirone (5 mg/per os) (Zuardi et al., 1993). Recently, in view of its anxiolytic effect, neuroimaging studies were performed to test whether CBD was able to affect neural functioning in brain regions usually implicated in the pathophysiology of anxiety. The findings demonstrated that CBD modulates neuronal activity in limbic and paralimbic areas, including orbitofrontal, cingulate and medial temporal cortex, and the insula (Crippa et al., 2004).

In addition to anxiolytic actions, early investigations also demonstrated that CBD induces biphasic hypnotic effects in rats as well as enhances sleeping time, compared with placebo, in insomniacs (Monti, 1977; Carlini and Cunha, 1981).

However, more recent results from animal studies rendered controversial previous data, since i.c.v. injections of CBD increased the extracellular level of dopamine in rat nucleus accumbens, suggesting that CBD can improve alertness, and might be regarded, on the contrary, as a potential therapeutic tool in sleep disorders such as hypersomnias (Murillo-Rodríguez et al., 2006)

CBD and control of movement disorders Anecdotal evidence has suggested a potential beneficial role of CBD, alone or in combination with Δ9-THC, in different neurodegenerative diseases, including Parkinson's disease (PD) and Huntington's disease (HD), two chronic illnesses due to degenerative processes involving specific nuclei of the basal ganglia, resulting in the abnormal regulation of movements. Both disorders have been scantly investigated from the clinical point of view, whereas, at the preclinical level, the accumulated findings appear more exhaustive and convincing for the possible medical utilization of CBD to improve symptoms and/ or delay disease progression. According to recent preclinical findings, plant-derived cannabinoids were able to prevent neuronal damage induced by 6-hydroxydopamine unilateral injection into the nigra, pars compacta (LastresBecker et al., 2005). This effect appeared not to implicate CB receptor mediation while, more likely, it might be due to antioxidant activity, possibly combined with the capability to modulate glial responses, relevant to neural survival. In rats with hemiparkinsonism, generated by the nigral administration of 6-hydroxydopamine, the neuroprotective effects exerted by CBD reverted dopaminergic transmission impairment, by reducing dopaminergic cell death, rather than by enhancing the functional turnover of the surviving neurons (LastresBecker et al., 2005).

Early human reports demonstrated a dose-related improvement (ranging from 20% to 50%) in parkinsonian patients treated with oral doses of CBD (100–600 mg/day over a 6 week period) (Consroe et al., 1986). Conversely, in a more recent controlled trial of a mixture of Δ9-THC/CBD (2.5 mg/1.25 mg per capsule), it failed to exert any beneficial effect either on parkinsonism or levodopa-induced dyskinesias (Caroll et al., 2004).

Unfortunately no subsequent trials were performed in an attempt to clarify such conflicting results. Certainly, in comparison with the relevance of preclinical data, the limited clinical evidence suggests that human studies should be carried out to verify for good the potential for a future clinical application of CBD in PD. Similarly, based on anecdotal accounts and the results of preliminary clinical observations CBD was considered to be a compound with therapeutic potential also against hyperkinetic disorders. Indeed, CBD was demonstrated to mitigate apomorphine-induced turning behaviour in 6-hydroxydopamine injected rats, an animal model of hyperkinetic movement disorders, while, on the other hand, it was able to potentiate hypokinesia generated by tetrabenazine (Consroe et al., 1988). More recently CBD was found to protect striatal neurons against the in vivo toxicity of 3-nitropropionic acid, a mitochondrial toxin that replicates some biochemical alterations occurring in HD (Sagredo et al., 2007).

Cannabidiol was investigated for its efficacy in HD, alone or as an add-on drug to the approved therapy with neuroleptics (Consroe et al., 1991b). CBD, at an average daily dose of 10 mg/kg/day for 6 weeks, was neither symptomatically effective nor toxic compared with placebo, in neuroleptic-free patients with HD.

Considering the negative results on both the therapeutic and the safety measures, there is a question about the dose as well as the duration of the trial. Since these results cannot be considered conclusive, further trials, utilizing CBD alone or in combination with Δ9-THC, should be performed to evaluate clinically the real antihyperkinetic value of these molecules.

Amyotrophic lateral sclerosis (ALS) is a fatal neurodegenerative disease characterized by selective loss involving motoneuronal cells in the cortex, brainstem and spinal cord. Recent reports confirm that in the pathophysiology of ALS neuroinflammation and oxidative stress play a crucial role (Turner and Talbot, 2008). Based on this evidence, it is possible to speculate that CBD, because of its antinflammatory and antioxidative properties, could be a promising option to improve disturbances and prolong survival in ALS patients. This is strongly reinforced by the observations that Δ9-THC was able to delay impairment and prolong survival in a mouse transgenic model of ALS, and that similar results were achieved when cannabinol was used (Weydt et al., 2005). Furthermore, these findings have to be considered together with anecdotal reports that recreational smoking of marijuana does improve symptomatology in ALS subjects.

CBD and experimental model of Alzheimer diseases To date very promising results have been achieved in the control of β-amyloid (Aβ) toxicity by utilizing CBD.

Although at present it is still not fully clear the precise biochemical mechanisms by which Aβ exerts its detrimental effects, nevertheless its role in inducing neuronal damage and in mediating neuroinflammation. Following this idea, it has been demonstrated that CBD protected differentiated PC12 neuronal cells from Aβ exposure, through a combination of antioxidant, antiinflammatory and antiapoptotic effects (Iuvone et al., 2004). The CBD antioxidant effect accounts mainly for the survival of cultured neurons, with a potency higher than α-tocopherol.

Moreover it helps to attenuate Aβ neurotoxicity, even with a mechanism not possessed by classical antioxidants. In fact, CBD administration results in a blunting of Aβ- induced GSK-3β activation, the key enzyme of the WNT/ β-catenin pathway, so preventing the hyperphosphorylation of tau proteins and, consequently, neurofibrillary tangle formation.

Cannabidiol decreases the phosphorylation of the stressactivated protein kinase, P38 MAPK, so preventing translocation to the nucleus of NF-κB and the subsequent transcription of important pro-inflammatory genes, including that encoding for iNOS protein (Esposito et al., 2006). The CBD antiinflammatory properties were also confirmed in an in vivo study on mice inoculated with Aβ, where CBD dose-dependently inhibited reactive gliosis, by impairing glial cell activation and proinflammatory mediator release (Esposito et al., 2007).

Despite these encouraging preclinical results, the therapeutic potential of CBD in AD is already being investigated. Clinical trials to explore the beneficial effects of Δ9-THC/CBD mixture in AD patients are presently in progress.

CONCLUSION

Cannabidiol exhibits an impressive plethora of actions, including anticonvulsive, sedative, hypnotic, antipsychotic, antiinflammatory and neuroprotective properties.

Many of which may be of therapeutic relevance as well as serving as leads for pharmaceutical development.

CBD is a compound well tolerated in humans, with a profile of very low toxicity, and devoid of psychoactive and cognitive effects. Preliminary studies highlight these remarkably important properties and encourage further experiments to be performed in more complex systems in order to clarify the mechanism(s) responsible for its molecular and cellular actions. At the same time, since most of the investigations suggesting CBD as a novel medicine with substantial neuroprotective potential have been carried out in the most part in animal or then cellular models, then more clinical trials able to validate its beneficial properties are warranted.

The results generated by these trials might allow that the current promising expectatives can progress from the present preclinical evidence to a practical therapeutic application.

In the last 45 years it has been possible to demonstrate that CBD has a wide range of pharmacological effects, many of which being of great therapeutic interest, but still waiting to be confirmed by clinical trials.

It is important to highlight that many effects of CBD draw a bell-shaped dose-response curve, suggesting that the dose is a pivotal factor in CBD research. The wide range of CBD effects can be explained by the multiple mechanisms through which CBD acts, although further research is needed to clarify the precise mechanisms that underlie some of the potentially beneficial effects of CBD.

Thank you again for buying this book!

I hope this book will help you to understand the benefits of using CBD Hemp Oil.

Printed in Great Britain
by Amazon